Centaurs

by
Rebecca Phillips-Bartlett

Minneapolis, Minnesota

Credits

All images are courtesy of Shutterstock.com, unless otherwise specified. With thanks to Getty Images, Thinkstock Photo, iStockphoto, and Adobe Stock.

Recurring – vectortatu, Macrovector. Cover – Vector_Vision. 2–3 – Daria_Art, delcarmat. 4–5 – tomertu, TimeImage Production, Natalllenka.m, mountain beetle. 6–7 – Sammy33, FARBAI, Antonio. 8–9 – Tarakanbix, Daniel Eskridge, Дина Попова, David. 10–11 – Warm_Tail, Salinee_Chot, emyerson, Hoika Mikhail. 12–13 – Daniel Eskridge, Macrovector, Danilo Sanino, galina ermolaeva. 14–15 – Morphart Creation. 16–17 – Fotokostic, mariait, Matt Gibson, TreesTons. 18–19 – MDV Edwards, Kazakova Maryia, Fona. 20–21 – KOSTAS TSEK, Algol, nutriaaa. 22–23 – PeopleImages.com - Yuri A , Przemek Klos.

Bearport Publishing Company Product Development Team
Publisher: Jen Jenson; Director of Product Development: Spencer Brinker; Managing Editor: Allison Juda; Editor: Cole Nelson; Associate Editor: Naomi Reich; Associate Editor: Tiana Tran; Art Director: Colin O'Dea; Designer: Kim Jones; Designer: Kayla Eggert; Product Development Specialist: Owen Hamlin

Library of Congress Cataloging-in-Publication Data is available at www.loc.gov or upon request from the publisher.

ISBN: 979-8-89232-739-8 (hardcover)
ISBN: 979-8-89232-789-3 (paperback)
ISBN: 979-8-89232-826-5 (ebook)

© 2025 BookLife Publishing
This edition is published by arrangement with BookLife Publishing.

North American adaptations © 2025 Bearport Publishing Company. All rights reserved. No part of this publication may be reproduced in whole or in part, stored in any retrieval system, or transmitted in any form or by any means, electronic, mechanical, photocopying, recording, or otherwise, without written permission from the publisher.

For more information, write to Bearport Publishing, 5357 Penn Avenue South, Minneapolis, MN 55419.

CONTENTS

Myths, Magic, and More. **4**
What Does a Centaur Look Like? **6**
A Fighting Beast **8**
Magical Powers **10**
This and That **12**
Chiron. **14**
Where Centaurs Live **16**
Mythical Look-Alikes **18**
Real-Life Centaurs? **20**
Mysterious Mythical Creatures **22**
Glossary **24**
Index **24**

MYTHS, MAGIC, AND MORE

You may have heard of the half-human, half-horse creatures known as centaurs (SEN-torz). But you probably haven't seen one in real life. Why not? Because centaurs are **mythical** creatures!

For thousands of years, people from all over the world have told stories about centaurs. Different **legends** talk about the creatures in different ways. Let's learn what the stories have to say!

Stories about centaurs go as far back as **ancient** Greece.

WHAT DOES A CENTAUR LOOK LIKE?

Let's take a closer look at these four-legged creatures.

Upper body

The upper body of a centaur looks like a human.

Lower body

Their lower half looks like a horse.

A FIGHTING BEAST

Centaurs have both horselike hooves and human hands.

Hooves are supposed to be one of the centaur's strongest weapons. Like donkeys, could the creatures deliver a powerful backward kick?

Centaurs are thought to use their human hands to fight. In some stories, they use their strong grip to hold tree branches. Other stories say centaurs battle with bows and arrows.

Most **primates** have five fingers on their hands.

MAGICAL POWERS

Apart from their fighting abilities, what else have we heard about these mythical creatures? Centaurs in legends are magical.

Some stories say centaurs have the ability to see the future. This type of magic is called divination. Fortune tellers are said to have this power, too.

Could centaurs have other powers? Possibly! In legends, one centaur knew how to create a special **medicine** to **heal** others.

THIS AND THAT

Ancient Greek stories say the very first centaur was born from a cloud. But this wasn't just any cloud . . . It was a cloud made by a god named Zeus.

Zeus

Zeus was the god of the sky and thunder.

What would a half-human, half-horse eat? Some stories say centaurs eat bread and fruits. These foods are also eaten by both humans and horses.

Some legends tell of **violent** centaurs. These stories may be trying to tell a **moral**. They warn people against losing control and becoming wild.

CHIRON

Not all the tales are about violent centaurs. A centaur called Chiron (KYE-ruhn) was believed to be very wise and kind.

Chiron

In stories, Chiron showed what could happen if people controlled their wild sides. This taught readers about the world and how to help others.

During his long life, Chiron studied many different things. He learned about the stars and medicine. Then, Chiron passed on his knowledge to other heroes and gods.

Asclepius

Chiron was said to have taught Asclepius, the Greek god of medicine.

WHERE CENTAURS LIVE

As creatures of ancient Greek myths, most centaurs were said to be found in northern Greece. Maybe they lived in forests and mountains. Stories say centaurs made their homes out of branches and leaves.

Some legends say centaurs lived on the mountains of Thessaly and Arcadia in ancient Greece.

Centaurs are thought to live in groups. This might help keep them safe.

MYTHICAL LOOK-ALIKES

There are other mythical creatures like centaurs. Let's look at a few.

A tikbalang

Like a centaur, a tikbalang (TIK-ba-luhng) is a half-human, half-horse creature. It has a horse's head and hooves, but a tikbalang's torso looks human.

Ichthyocentaurs (ick-thee-uh-SEN-torz) are similar to centaurs. But what makes them different? These creatures have fish tails!

A faun

An ichthyocentaur

A faun (FAWN) is similar to a centaur. But instead of part horse, it is part goat. Many stories say this mythical being likes to make music.

REAL-LIFE CENTAURS?

Where do the stories of centaurs come from? Maybe from real-life animals....

Horse Riders

People have been riding horses for more than 5,000 years. When people first saw other humans riding, they may have thought they were centaurs!

Horses

Horse heads are sometimes mistaken as human torsos. Like centaurs, horse hooves keep their toes safe while they run.

Deer

Perhaps deer could have been mistaken for centaurs. In stories, some centaurs have horns.

MYSTERIOUS MYTHICAL CREATURES

Centaurs are fun, mysterious creatures. We can learn a lot from stories about these wild beasts.

If you can't get enough of centaurs, just read some books! There is so much to explore about these magical, mythical creatures.

GLOSSARY

ancient belonging to a time long ago

heal to become healthy again

legends stories from the past that may have a mix of truth and made-up things

medicine something that is used to treat an illness or pain

moral a story intended to teach a lesson

mythical based on stories or something made up in the imagination

myths old stories that tell of strange or magical events and creatures

primates members of the group of animals that include humans, monkeys, and apes

violent especially harmful or destructive

INDEX

animals 20
Chiron 14–15
forests 16
Greece 5, 12, 15–16
hooves 7–8, 18, 21
horns 7, 21
horses 4, 6, 8, 13, 18, 20–21
mountains 16
myths 7, 16
Zeus 12

24